DON'T YOU DARE TOUCH ME THERE!!

by Kandra Albury

Copyright © 2013 by Kandra Albury

All rights reserved. No part of this publication may be reproduced, distributed, or transmitted in any form or by any means, including photocopying, recording, or other electronic or mechanical methods, without the prior written permission of the publisher, except in the case of brief quotations embodied in critical reviews and certain other noncommercial uses permitted by copyright law.

Books may be ordered through online retailers or by contacting:

Kandra Albury
www.kandraalbury.org

Illustrated by Jamie Cosley
www.jamiecosley.com

ISBN: 978-0-692-93998-7

Dedication

I dedicate this book to all children. My mission is to give one of God's greatest blessings a voice in today's noisy world. Special thank you to my husband James and my children for their support and believing in me and this project that I hold close to my heart.

Thank you Jamie Cosley for the super job on the illustrations.

I am confident children around the globe will be empowered to stand up for themselves and tell when someone is touching them inappropriately.

Courageously yours,
Kandra

Courageous Cody

Age: 6 (birthday August 25th)

Grade: First

Favorite subject: Math

Favorite food: Pizza

Favorite color: Orange

Hobbies: Playing with his cat Cotton and his friend Daring Diego

Daring Diego

Age: 7 (birthday September 6th)

Grade: Second

Favorite subject: Science

Favorite food: Peanut butter and jelly sandwich (crust removed)

Favorite color: Blue

Hobbies: Looking for bugs outside and playing with his friend Courageous Cody

MEET THE FEISTY FOUR!!

Sassy Simone
Age: 5 ½ (birthday July 29th)
Grade: Kindergarten
Favorite subject: Spelling
Favorite food: Macaroni and cheese
Favorite color: Green
Hobbies: Trying on her mommy's earrings, playing with her dog Oreo and her friend Karate-chop Kimmy

Karate-chop Kimmy
Age: 7 (birthday February 19th)
Grade: Second
Favorite subject: Reading
Favorite food: Spaghetti and meatballs
Favorite color: Red
Hobbies: Playing dress up with her friend Sassy Simone and practicing her karate moves

TOUCHING CAN MAKE YOU HAPPY.

TOUCHING CAN MAKE YOU SAD.

TICKLES AND HUGS ARE JUST FINE,

BUT DON'T YOU DARE

TOUCH MY BEHIND!

YOU CAN BE MY FRIEND AND GIVE ME HIGH FIVES

1

PERHAPS A LITTLE KISS ON MY FOREHEAD WILL DO.

MAYBE YOU CARE
AND I'M GLAD YOU DO,
BUT IF YOU DARE TOUCH
ME THERE, I'M GOING
TO TELL ON YOU!

OK, YOU CAN RUB
MY HEAD FOR A JOB
WELL DONE,
BUT BAD TOUCHING
WILL RUIN THE FUN!

16

GROWN-UPS ARE SUPPOSED TO BE TRUSTED. BUT IF YOU DARE TOUCH ME THERE, YOU WILL GET BUSTED!

18

WELL I MIGHT
BE LITTLE
BUT I'M NO FOOL!

'CAUSE IF YOU DARE TOUCH ME **THERE, THERE OR THERE** IT WON'T BE COOL!

BAD TOUCHING ISN'T HEALTHY AND IT'S JUST NOT RIGHT! I MAY NOT BE AS STRONG AS YOU ARE BUT I'LL PUT UP ONE HECK OF A FIGHT!

YEAH, I'M GOING TO TELL AND SING LIKE A BIRD!
IF YOU DON'T KNOW, YOU BETTER ACT LIKE YOU HEARD!

YOU THINK I'M A PUSH OVER? BETTER THINK AGAIN BECAUSE I WILL TELL ANOTHER FAMILY MEMBER, ADULT OR FRIEND!

I WON'T FEEL
EMBARRASSED,
'CAUSE I'M NOT
THE ONE TO BLAME,

IF YOU MAKE ME
FEEL UNCOMFORTABLE
THE LEAST LITTLE BIT,

IF SOMEONE IS HURTING ME, WHETHER IT'S A FRIEND OR A STRANGER, I PROMISE TO ALWAYS TELL WHEN I FEEL I'M IN DANGER!

32

YES, I'M GOING TO STAND UP FOR MYSELF AND OTHERS TOO AND TELL, TELL, TELL ......TELL ON YOU!!

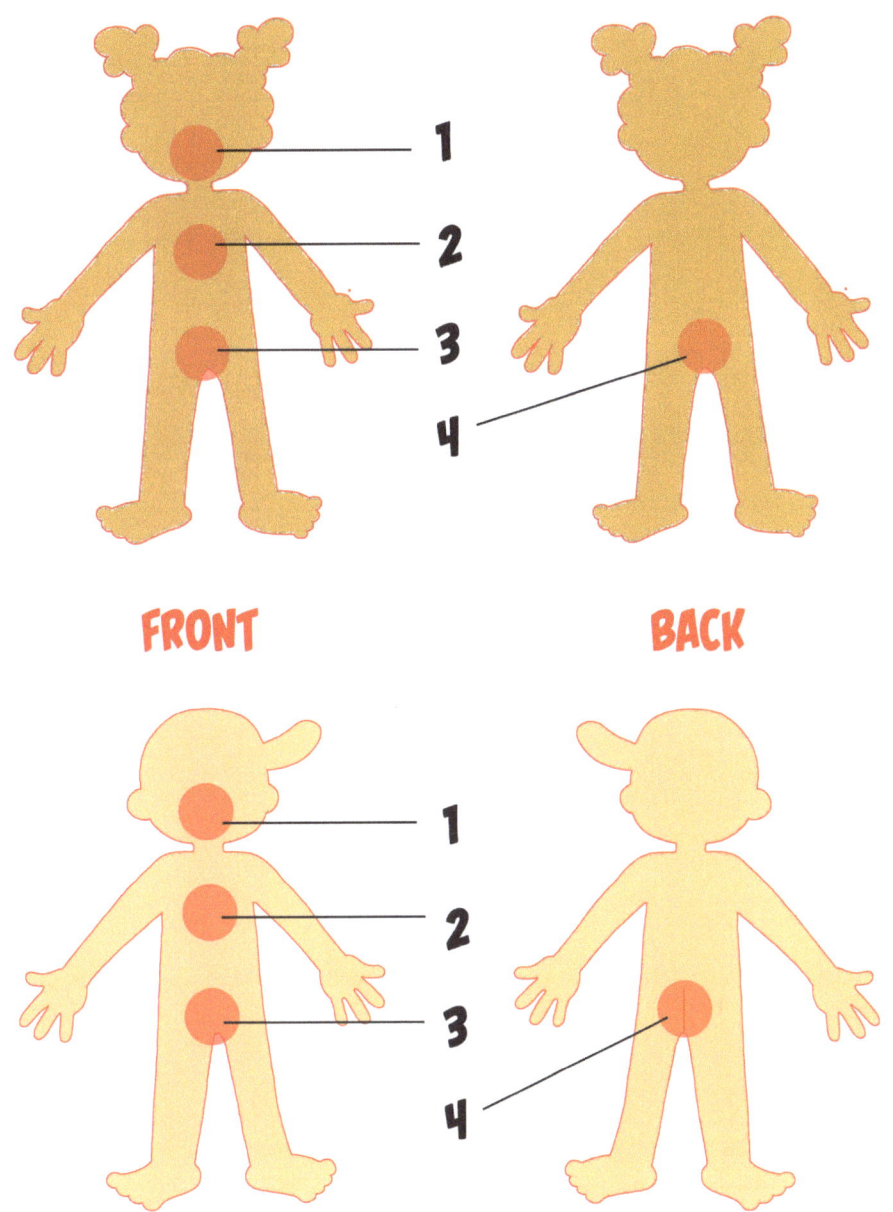

Learning about the **Don't You Dare Touch Me There Zones** ™ (DYDTMTZ) can be a serious yet fun experience. Here are some tips to start the courage conversation.

Parents, first, let your kid-sized superhero know these areas are absolutely private* and are typically covered by a swimsuit or bath towel. Zones two, three and four should not be touched or photographed.

There are four zones:

Zone 1: Mouth- Only something to eat or drink goes here. Sometimes you may not feel well and a responsible adult may have to give you medication to help you feel better. So what's your favorite food? What is your least favorite food? Have a favorite fruit or vegetable?

Zone 2: Chest for boys or breast area for girls.

Zone 3: What's in front: Genital area.

Zone 4: Buttocks or bottom

*Parents, be sure to call these areas by name and teach your kid-sized superhero to wash these areas on their own during bath time. Reassure your child that they can always tell you anything. Until next time, be courageous!

The Promise to Tell and Listen Agreement

I (child's name) _____ promise to always tell an adult when someone is hurting me or makes me feel uncomfortable.

I/we (parent/guardian's name) _____ promise to always listen and take immediate action when my child tells me that someone is hurting him/her.

Today's date _____

DON'T YOU DARE TOUCH ME THERE! DISCUSSION QUESTIONS

Encourage students to turn up the volume on their ears! ☺ This will help them to use active listening skills as the story is being read.

1. What is the title of the book? **Answer: "Don't You Dare Touch Me There!"**

   Have the kids repeat the title in unison.

2. Why do you think the "Feisty Four" (the four characters) wear capes? **Answer: Because they are heroes/they can protect themselves/others.**

3. What is this book about? **Answer: Bad/unhealthy or inappropriate touching and telling when someone makes you feel uncomfortable or touches you in a bad way.**

   Remind children that <u>no one</u> is touch them in areas that their bathing suit covers or on parts of their body that they cover with a bath towel, and they should <u>not</u> touch others in those areas either. Also remind them that their mouth is also a private part.

4. Give some examples of good touch from the book. **Answer: High 5, head rub, a kiss to the forehead, a pat on the back, or a hug.** Explain that good touch gets a thumbs up.

   Remind children that if touching makes them sad, cry, uncomfortable or if it hurts, it is <u>BAD</u> touch (pg. 4). Explain that bad touch equals a thumbs down.

5. Who is Daring Diego giving a High 5 to on page 8? **Answer: His grandpa.**

6. Diego says, "I'm not down with that bad touching jive." on pg. 9.

   Explain that if someone wants to play a touching game and they don't like it. They can say "Don't You Dare Touch Me There!" Or, "Stop, I don't like that game!"

For additional tools, visit **kandraalbury.org/**

DON'T YOU DARE TOUCH ME THERE! DISCUSSION QUESTIONS

7. What is the name of Sassy Simone's dog? **Answer: Oreo (because it's the colors of Oreo cookies). Ask the kids (by a show of hands) if they like Oreo cookies!**

8. What is the name of Courageous Cody's cat? **Answer: Cotton (because the cat is fluffy)**

9. Courageous Cody says he will tell "lickety-split" if someone makes him feel uncomfortable. What does lickety-split mean? **Answer: Really fast, quickly or in a hurry!**

10. What is Karate-chop Kimmy doing on page 12? **Answer: Running really fast to tell!**

    One of Karate-chop Kimmy's hobbies is practicing her Karate moves. She uses her hands as stop signs to protect her "Don't You Dare Touch Me There Zones", and they can too!

11. What does Sassy Simone have in her hand on page 14? **Answer: A megaphone. She is using her voice to yell and tell.**

12. What is Courageous Cody doing on page 26? **Answer: Telling!**

13. Who is Courageous Cody telling on page 32? **Answer: A police officer.**

14. Who else can you tell if and/or when someone makes you feel sad, uncomfortable or is hurting you? **Answer: Another family member, adult, friend, teacher, principal, guidance counselor, etc.**

For additional tools, visit **kandraalbury.org/**

Draw a picture of yourself in a courageous superhero pose!
(Don't forget your cape!)

Make sure you share your drawing on the Kids'N Capes Facebook page!
facebook.com/CourageIsTheNewSuperpower/

FEISTY FOUR COLORING SHEET
COURAGEOUS CODY

For additional printable coloring sheets, visit **kandraalbury.org/just-4-kids**

FEISTY FOUR COLORING SHEET
DARING DIEGO

For additional printable coloring sheets, visit **kandraalbury.org/just-4-kids**

FEISTY FOUR COLORING SHEET
SASSY SIMONE

For additional printable coloring sheets, visit **kandraalbury.org/just-4-kids**

FEISTY FOUR COLORING SHEET
KARATE CHOP KIMMY

For additional printable coloring sheets, visit **kandraalbury.org/just-4-kids**

FEISTY FOUR COLORING SHEET
MEET THE FEISTY 4

For additional printable coloring sheets, visit **kandraalbury.org/just-4-kids**

FEISTY FOUR COLORING SHEET
MEET THE FEISTY 4

For additional printable coloring sheets, visit **kandraalbury.org/just-4-kids**

www.ingramcontent.com/pod-product-compliance
Lightning Source LLC
Chambersburg PA
CBHW042348300426
44110CB00032B/68